About the Editor

Poet and publisher **Ronnie Goodyer** is Poet-in-Residence for the League Against Cruel Sports and runs Indigo Dreams Publishing with partner Dawn Bauling. Indigo Dreams won the Most Innovative Publisher Award in 2017 and 2021, the only publisher to have been awarded this on two occasions.

He established his own Celebrity Management company in the 1980s and, among others, published Uri Geller's first novel *Shawn* and England cricketer-turned artist Jack Russell's *A Cricketer's Art*. Ronnie was on the BBC Judging Panel for their *Off By Heart* competition. aired on BBC2.

He has had seven collections of his poetry published, won many competitions and, with Dawn, won the Ted Slade Award for Services to Poetry. This is given to honour people who have made a significant impact in the poetry world and have published poets who would not have otherwise found an outlet for their work.

A strong supporter of animal rights and the natural world, Ronnie is extremely proud to be Poet-in-Residence for the League Against Cruel Sports, raising awareness wherever he can.

He lives with Dawn and their rescue blue merle collie Mist in an ex-forester's house in the rural southwest of England.

The League Against Cruel Sports

The League Against Cruel Sports is proud to be part of this, the second anthology of poems entitled *Voices For The Silent*. The title says it all, as the many animals needlessly persecuted for entertainment need to be heard. Poetry gives them a voice they so richly deserve.

Campaigning to end cruel animal sports should be easy in the year 2022. Yet, despite the overwhelming opposition to it across the United Kingdom, it is not. Rather it is expensive, skilled, and laborious work as we seek to overturn centuries of animal cruelty, perpetrated by those with the power to keep these practices going. We do not receive any government funding to do this, and we rely entirely on the generosity of our supporters.

It is therefore with great pride that we send our sincere thanks for supporting us by buying this anthology. We assure you that every penny really does count in helping us to protect animals from being harmed or killed in the name of sport. Step by step, we are winning more and more protections for animals. United, we are redefining what is acceptable and giving animals the voice they deserve.

Indigo Dreams, publishers of *Voices For The Silent*, have kindly undertaken this venture with and to benefit the League through a Charity Partnership Agreement with profits being paid to the League from each book sold. We are delighted to count this as our second anthology in our 98-year history, building on the success of the first. We would like to express our heartfelt thanks to Indigo Dreams, especially to their editor and League's Poet-In-Residence **Ronnie Goodyer**, for the difference they are making to animal welfare.

If you'd like to get involved further in our work or learn more please visit www.league.org.uk or call our Supporter Care Team on 01483 524 250 or email supportercare@league.org.uk

Thank you for supporting us by purchasing *Voices For The Silent.*

With kind regards
Andy Knott MBE, CEO
and all at the League.
United, we will end animal cruelty in the name of sport

Indigo Dreams and the League Against Cruel Sports would like to thank the following supporters for their special contribution to the creation of this anthology.

Dorothy Allan

Dawn Bauling

Brian Craig

Vivien Foulkes-James

Victoria Gatehouse

Michael Gray

Gabriel Griffin

Deborah Harvey

Mark Haworth-Booth

Ian Huckson

Sally King

Emma Lord

Dru Marland

Frank McMahon

Jan Moran Neil

David Norris-Kay

Terry Quinn

Chrys Salt

Jane Smith

Hannah Stone

Linda Tilbury

Mick Yates

A few words from Ronnie...

"Of all the paths you take in life, make sure a few of them are dirt." — **John Muir**

Following the success of *For The Silent,* the first poetry anthology in the League Against Cruel Sports' history, I felt the time was right to create and publish a second anthology, *Voices For The Silent.* The response was wonderful, so many poets wishing to support the cause, so many encouraging emails. The process was a long, sometimes frustrating one, delayed by research, selection, permission requests – and two bouts of covid!

This anthology is enhanced by the artwork of Sam Cannon and photography of Andy Parkinson, and I can't thank them enough for their enthusiasm and the helpful support they have given to me. Do visit their websites, they are enchanting!

Included are poems that highlight the plight of and the cruelty to animals. There are others that embrace the beauty of wildlife and nature, the threat that some of them are under. I thank all poets included for their contribution, which will assist the League Against Cruel Sports in their constant fight against animal cruelty.

Huge thanks also to Sophie Baden at the League who's a pleasure to work with. And a special mention to my partner, Dawn Bauling, for shouldering some extra responsibilities with Indigo Dreams' very busy schedule while I progressed this project. I may be reminded of that from time to time!

Ronnie Goodyer
Editor

Sam Cannon

Sam is a UK based artist who combines her loves of typography, calligraphy and wildlife.

At her home in Dorset she is trying to create a home for wildlife, encouraging both mammals and insects and giving them a place where they are safe all year round. She is lucky enough to have 8 acres to experiment with (mostly by letting the fields and hedgerows 'just be').

All of these influences become a rich source of inspiration for her paintings, as are the local seaside towns of Dorset.

Sam's prints and card can be found in shops and galleries around the UK. She also has an online shop https://samcannonart.co.uk

Sam can also be found on Instagram, Facebook and Twitter @samcannonart

If you are unfamiliar with Sam's work and merchandise (I've been buying Sam's card/calendars for years) then please visit the links shown above, it's guaranteed to lighten your day.

Andy Parkinson

Andy Parkinson is a feature contributor to National Geographic magazine, a Nikon Europe Ambassador (Wildlife) and is one of Europe's most awarded photographers. With more than 100 individual awards, his photographs feature consistently in all the world's most prestigious wildlife photographic competitions.

In 2020 he was named the overall winner of one of the world's most prestigious conservation photography prizes, the Big Picture Natural World, and in 2016 he was named the overall winner of Bird Photographer of the Year. He has been given awards 4 times in Wildlife Photographer of the Year, 5 times in European Wildlife Photographer of the Year, whilst in 2012 he was named the Nature Photojournalist of the Year for a portfolio of 12 gannet images captured whilst working on assignment for National Geographic magazine.

He now spends most of his year organising and leading photographic adventures to some of the most spectacular destinations on Earth.

Andy's website is www.andrewparkinson.com and Instagram
https://www.instagram.com/andyparkinsonphoto/?hl=en

CONTENTS

Voices For The Silent

At night I dream that you & I are two trees
that grew together, roots entwined,
& that you know the earth & the rain like my mouth,
since we are made of earth & rain.
- **Pablo Neruda**

Rebirth on the Mystic Moor – Ronnie Goodyer

New birdsong in this bracken-oak
New gold upon the distant tor
And peeling back the hunters' choke
There's rebirth on the mystic moor
The dew-soaked, deer-cloaked, mystic moor

The dog-fox darting out to greet it
River's water angel-bright
Penetrating darkness underneath it
Rainbow flows of freefall light
Earth-fed, birth-red, freefall light

Running now by gorse and hawthorn
Spitting its spray at vixen yawning
Passing the buck and doe and fawn
It clicks the keys of this new dawn morning
Spray-making, day-breaking, new dawn morning

So leave the troubles of mankind
And follow me from moor to sea
Here there is a soul to find
Join the dawn and join it free
New gold upon the distant tor
There's rebirth on the mystic moor

*During Covid restrictions/lockdown the countryside developed naturally
again, the birdsong louder, deer and fox more visible, living natural lives as
is their birthright.*

Observing the Stag – Ronnie Goodyer

Observing the stag as he's chased through his homeland
by a relay of hounds and adrenalized hunters;
hour upon hour, until completely exhausted,
terrified by the sounds, the scents and the numbers.

Observing the stag, his spirit now broken,
no breath left for running, no will left to fight;
standing at bay as the gunman approaches –
one shot marks the fun-filled end of his life.

Observing the stag as it falls from the killing;
delight at the death on this wonderful day.
The hunters, the liggers and pay-to-view followers,
all morally bankrupt whatever they pay.

Observing the law with its loopholes to kill through
and wildlife campaigners who'll force changes to come.
When one day the stag won't be hunted and slaughtered
And the shot from the camera will replace the gun.

Stag hunts claim exemption under the Research and Observation loophole in much the same way the Japanese Government claim that they are killing whales for research. Three hunts are currently chasing and killing red deer: Devon and Somerset Staghounds in Exmoor National Park; Quantock Staghounds on Quantock and Brendon Hills: Tiverton Staghounds hunting the Exe, Taw and Torridge valleys.

The Mower – Philip Larkin

The mower stalled, twice; kneeling, I found
A hedgehog jammed up against the blades,
Killed. It had been in the long grass.

I had seen it before, and even fed it, once.
Now I had mauled its unobtrusive world
Unmendably. Burial was no help:

Next morning I got up and it did not.
The first day after a death, the new absence
Is always the same; we should be careful

Of each other, we should be kind
While there is still time.

From *Collected Poems*. Reprinted by permission of Faber and Faber Ltd
and the Estate of Philip Larkin

Driving with Animals – Billy Collins

I drive this road that whips through woods at night
always searching ahead for the reflective eyes of deer
who will venture onto the grassy verge to browse.

Winter-snug in the warm interior of the car,
I am speeding in the vague nowhere between places,
an arithmetic problem in space and time
which passes slowly on this long solo haul.
I feed cassettes into the dash, light cigarettes,
check the softly lit panel of instruments
measuring motion, pressure, heat, the arcana of the engine,
but there is no red needle to indicate deer.

If I drill my eyes into the night long enough
I will hallucinate shapes in pockets of darkness,
not only deer peering from the fringe of trees,
but other anomalous animals: bison, zebra, even
fish floating in the dreamy pools of fog,

animals released from the mind's deep zoo,
animals we think we see in passing clouds
and in the connected dots of constellations.
Animals parading through the greenery of Eden,
animals on the turning pages of storybooks.
And always deer stepping from the sanctuary of woods,
bolting across the hard ribbon of road in shock,
locked in death-leaps in the sparkle of headlights.

At home as the motor cools in the driveway,
I will feel these rhythms in the quiet of the house.
I will see the heads of deer in the darkened bedroom
and a white flick of tail in the dresser mirror.
I will dream of the sensational touch of a buck's fur
and rock to sleep in the bow and lift of antlers.

From *Taking Off Emily Dickinson's Clothes* republished by kind permission Pan Macmillan

When the last wolf in Scotland was skinned – A C Clarke

stags perked antlers, sheep settled into their fleeces,
farmers stopped counting lambs into the night-fold.
The village sighed its gratitude.
Howling meant nothing now but the wind

whose claws might tear down chimneypots, smash slates,
but not draw blood. The woods opened for trysts.
Children played there fearing no worse than brambles.
The old stories shrank from warning

to fireside tales. Soon no-one alive
had seen a wolf in the Scottish wilds.
Then fences rose above the height of a deer-leap.
Marksmen trained their sights on ageing hinds

that would not have outrun a hunting pack.
Each year they killed. Each year the herds increased.
Forests grew thin, creatures that used to hide there
disappeared. Roads battered through.

Dogwalkers followed, tugged by weak imitations
of fierce forebears. Hikers. Cyclists.
Foragers raided toadstools, wild garlic.
Trees marched in dark green files.

The last wolfskin has passed into legend.
A hunter staked it to the heartwood
of the church where he praised God every Sunday
for all His glorious Creation.

Skylark – Fiona Ritchie Walker

Like apple, cream, crumble, spread on a restaurant plate,
see how we have deconstructed you,
storing your call as a ringtone rising from our pockets,
saving the video *skylark feeding young* to our favourites.

Alauda Arvensis
your song,
a sequence of actions.
We did not recognise
it meant flight or danger.

Your name now listed in threatened red,
lost territory marked on interactive maps,
fields too bare for your beak
to weave nests, clutch the future.

Our skies lie silent as Wikipedia waits
for your final line,
date of the last widely accepted sighting.

First published in *Counting Down the Days* (Grey Hen Press)

Once Upon a Time in the West Country – Louise Longson

He must have come to escape the gunfire.
A *desperado* dressed in dandy's plumage;
ring-necked renegade in flashy copper
coat-tails; green iridescence. Yellow
eyes stare, unblinking, behind the red
mask of a hardened *bandido*.

He takes over the joint. He guzzles
and gobbles; he has sized up the opposition.
The saloon-door-slap of his wings, the klaxon-cackle
 of his takeover sends the others flying.
Unassailable *machismo*.

And then his women come. Attracted
by his territorial rasp of sex.
They are plump, pretty; pale in comparison;
a *frou-frou* of cinnamon and beige petticoats
skittering after him.

After a few weeks, they are gone;
leaving behind a trail of spoiled seed beds, empty
food stores and shit. A gradual peace returns.
Only the distant rumble of rifles reminds us
an uncivil war still wages.

First published in *Reach Poetry* (Indigo Dreams)

Missing you already – Chrys Salt

Time was we'd find
gloomy pop-eyed presences
in damp dung coloured corners of dead leaves,
cup warty panting bellies in hot hands;
find marvellous gold cords
coiled behind corrugated iron
to muscle round our fingers,
and slide through;
watch pig-mouse snouts
on slug hunts
whiffle round flowerpots at dusk,
splayed quills and tiny bones,
tattooed in tyre tracks,
evidence of tribes.
Trapezing athletes, russet in the sun
feasting on garden feeders upside down;
jelly dollops beached by tides,
the sideways disappearing acts
in sodden sand;
blood spattered massacres on glass,
legs snapped by wipers;
striped furry nuzzlers
in nasturtium mouths so few,
a toxic legacy of legions lost
for future generations to download-
the hedgehog with the dinosaur,
the bumble bee, the toad.

Ticket To Ride – Philip Burton

Here is a brochure to introduce
the high speed train soon to devastate
England's green and pleasant heart
and satisfy the speed king in you.

Buzzard blood, the pigment suffused
in this leaflet, shouldn't deteriorate.
(Barn owl blood wouldn't be as colour-fast.
Crossbill blood might well strike through.)

And here is a badge of metallic blue
displaying the actual feathered nape
of a marsh tit, from the woods of Glyn Davies,
afixed with bluebell sap glue.

The old Cubbington pear tree we moved?
All that hooha concerning the fate
of England's *tree of the year*! Tout passe.
Attached are some pips we accrued.

Iseult of The White Hands has you
scurrying up from London on hot dates?
Deep in a social media app, you'll pass
subliminal traces of forest floor

and hardly know what's gone, or view
the Great Iron Way as laying waste
the forest of Morrois. Do not be aghast;
reduced journey times are a virtue.

Here is Derbyshire. So soon?
Two startled deer by the ruined gate,
Killamarsh Wood – a sunk Lyoness
in the oceans of time. Adieu. Adieu.

"Of all the animals, man is the only one that is cruel. He is the only one that inflicts pain for the pleasure of doing it." **Mark Twain**

Lily – Lisa Millard

Bred in captivity, held against
a will you never knew you had.
Suppressed by the suppressed,
an alien entity, not quite evolved but
compassion dissolved.

Moulded from mystical mist
you missed sunsets of peach
bliss and burnt nectarine sunrise.
A beauty lost in transmission
drowned in pointless 'tradition'

Blood wiped away with the swipe
of a greased palm, but they would
not devour you.

New tears still fall for anger,
cries still scream for injustice.
You rest peacefully, your soul, free.
We will never forget your name, Lily.

Dedicated to Lily the fox who was bred for a hunt and whose final moments were torture. She was nursed through her final breaths by a hunt sab and her body laid to rest.

Live Like A Winter Flowering Cherry – Chrissie Gittins

In the summer I'm unremarkable,
biding my time,
satisfied to let peonies and poppies take centre stage.
In autumn I begin to come into my own –
layering your lawn with
a daily tapestry of rust, orange, yellow.
When you've done clearing
and leaves lie only on your beds
to mulch against the cold
blossom spreads across my branches –
a filigree of black and pink
etched on chilly skies.
In the absence of snow,
my petals fall in flurries
covering your garden
in fragile flakes –
a scattering of light
glowing through the shortest days.

"Trees are poems the earth writes upon the sky,
We fell them down and turn them into paper,
That we may record our emptiness."
Kahlil Gibran

The Poplar Field – William Cowper

The poplars are felled, farewell to the shade
And the whispering sound of the cool colonnade:
The winds play no longer and sing in the leaves,
Nor Ouse on his bosom their image receives.

Twelve years have elapsed since I first took a view
Of my favourite field, and the bank where they grew,
And now in the grass behold they are laid,
And the tree is my seat that once lent me a shade.

The blackbird has fled to another retreat
Where the hazels afford him a screen from the heat;
And the scene where his melody charmed me before
Resounds with his sweet-flowing ditty no more.

My fugitive years are all hasting away,
And I must ere long lie as lowly as they,
With a turf on my breast and a stone at my head,
Ere another such grove shall arise in its stead.

'Tis a sight to engage me, if anything can,
To muse on the perishing pleasures of man;
Short-lived as we are, our enjoyments, I see,
Have a still shorter date, and die sooner than we.

Goodbye Old Friends – Ronnie Goodyer

It's just after 7 in the morning, walking with Mist
in a part of the forest we know really well.
We're passing the gulley where a black-booted
fox startled us both. We stared at each other
until it sloped forward and melted into the trees.

There are divots in the powdery soil where
squirrels secreted their winter food.
We have watched them scrape the top layer,
place breakfast in their mouth and scurry
with high-tail hurry to the waiting canopy.

We are treading the track between ferns,
their fronds waving a breeze we do not feel.
I cannot give the sound of walking shoes
on pine needles and generations of leaf,
but it is soft, it is comforting. It is lovely.

I cannot give the sound of the birds, singing
the morning with their cathedral of sound,
but are lifted with the notes when we enter
this glade by the old bridge, where the trees
have created a microcosm of forest life.

Come winter, heavy machines will grip each one,
slice the base, trim the branches, place on a pile.
The whole process will take seconds. The machine-tread
will rut the ground, brash cover it.
By next winter's end, they will be gone.

Gone too will be the forest understory
that we spring on, where fox melts,
where squirrels scurry.
The roar of wind the new song;
the sound of silence its partner...

Mast Year – Victoria Gatehouse

In a year that took so much,
the trees gave everything they had.

As you walked those solitary paths,
touched by the thin drizzle of spring,
conversations were happening between trees –

deep in the vaults between roots,
pale flickers across vast banks of darkness,
mychoroizzal whisperings,
a pledge that would bankrupt
for years to come
for this cache of hard mast -

gleaming shoals of beech-nuts,
cones, open-scaled in your hands
(a basket-full to brighten the fire)
the split gloss of conkers,
such bounty for squirrels, badgers, mice

and you -
looking up for a moment at a passing jay
an acorn in its beak,
blue-black jewels stitched into its wings.

In dreams
you're all feather, hollowed bone
throat and gullet packed with cupped fruit
as you journey to the scrublands
again and again -

your heart fit to burst, every acorn a gift
to be wrapped in the richness of soil
beneath tangled thickets
of blackthorn, bramble, gorse
those thorny guardians of saplings.

How everything comes back
to this wild taproot surge, thousands
of small crowns, lifting towards the light.

Winner *Indigo International Wild Nature Poetry Award 2021*

Tuscan Boars – Jenny Robb

i.

The noon air is heat and blood.
Hunters boast and smoke.
I glance through the open garage door,
flies buzz over sweet carcases;
their trotters glued to the floor
in dark red clotted pools.

ii.

An electric fence hums.
I gather acorns and stuff
them into my pockets,
clench them in my fists.

I hurl them over the fence.
Tons of boar pound through trees,
run to the scatter-shot sound of nuts
bouncing off baked earth.
I save some for the humbugs.
Snacks before their slaughter.

Digging – Dorothy Allan

Darkness is her element -
the scents of her surroundings.
She peeps her head outside
to snuffle in the leaf-mould.

Suddenly the sky lights up,
the quiet earth erupts in noise.
She knows that all is far from well –
yapping dogs and shouting men with spades
follow her retreat.

Her instinct is a hopeless fight
against an enemy she cannot see.
They advance with confidence
to take a helpless foe.

They are intent on slaughter
at no cost to themselves –
a fleeing fox, a badger stranded
underneath the ground,
a nation left defenceless
by broken promises of peace.

In Praise Of Badgers – Michael Newman

Again I hear the music of the spheres,
Watch Venus float away from stubborn clouds;
Again I quicken to the midnight hour,
And traipse the contoured fields round Dixton Wood.
I sense, not count, my shortened breaths, inspect
My torch for tinted cellophane. And wait.
This badger watch, relaxed, but midge-infested!
Cooled by breeze, I settle down, relate
To Badger Ballet, pas-de-snout. At risk
Of being ridiculed, I parody the Cull,
Rehearse my punchlines, then prepare in full
Such argument that common sense should whisk
Away all doubt. I had not reckoned, though,
With Ministry Jeeps, and men in white coats.

Encounter – Emma Lord

A wooden fence does not stem
the flow of white, cascading
over fields, to touch
the horizon where winter sky
meets frozen land.
Trees are silhouettes by day,
and by night. Each twisted branch
reaching towards watery
sunshine, which picks out
ice crystals in the snow.
A streak of red
darts from the woods
tears across the landscape.
Pauses
stares
orange eyes appraise me
across the distance.
Sensing no danger,
it continues its run
"Stay safe," I whisper
as the fox disappears,
auburn glow diminishing
within the trees
until I can see it no more.

Hare – Tina Negus

Hare running,
fleeing the dog, racing in fright
straight towards us, intent only on its pursuer,
eyes bulging, watching the excited hound.
Suddenly, it is aware of us, pauses,
leaps sideways, slips through the hedge.
Once in the field, it easily eludes the chaser,
sits on the skyline, watching,
washing its face.

Hare running,
jumping, leap-frogging its rival,
ears erect, forelimbs thrashing, flashing
in the fight.
Then they are off, careering in circles,
weaving patterns in the winter wheat,
full of the season,
mad hares, March hares.

Hare running,
lolloping over the stubble,
unhurried, thinking it is safe,
the man in the distance no threat,
no problem, no knowledge of guns
which kill from afar.
His world explodes in a puff of fur,
hind-legs kicking, in spasm,
in unconscious flight.

The dogs retrieve him,
the men lay him on the waiting trailer,
in rows, dead rows of his kith and kin.

The field is empty,
the hare is running
no more.

First published in *Sarasvati* magazine, Indigo Dreams

Obituary – Elsa Fischer

Iman has died
from her uterine tumours.

Her death has come sooner than expected.
There was no more the doctors could do

but they did obtain her egg cells for IVF.
Suffering from sudden blood loss

she'd escaped death a number of times.
Her forebears roamed across continents.

Of late she'd mostly kept
to herself, did not breed.

Men go for her horns.

Inspired by an article in The Guardian about Iman's death, she was the last existing Sumatra Rhino.

Luna's Skin – Christine Lowther

Luna the Orca 1999–2006

Whales are approaching
crossing the sky in heraldic procession
graceful zeppelins
our silent saviours
they sense the barrier between our species dissolving
they see the cedar boughs draped
over dugout canoes
they take in the flowers and bouquets of flowers
strewn over the wide surface of the water
tear-shaped petals scattered

Someone dives into the ocean looking for Luna:
a streaming skeleton surfaces,
whale-sized cave of bones emerging
but it is only the curved ribs of tree branches
barnacles clinging to grey cedar

We are always too late
smuggling in friendship
a clandestine love between species
expressed via touch
how else to soften the barrier
caress it into membrane:
in caring, we momentarily
perceive the other world
involuntarily
silence its music

In life, in the cold water,
Luna's skin was warm

Previously published in *My Nature* (Leaf Press, 2010, Vancouver Island).

In Meditation – Miranda Moon

silent in the space between breaths
perched on the next sound
inhale or chant
I hear bird song
my pause with their pause
we are united by our breath
mine yours theirs

with fox badger bird and deer
this land rises
in different sounds songs and shrieks
we people are not in concert
control from a self-appointed podium
seas of joy and suffering
course the years

the hare that runs free
does not pant or fret
but leaps and lands to rest
I have seen her there in height
glory sun on her brow
lifting her chest and paws to the final rays

the clear bugle calls a comfort song
says leave arrogance from our voice
use words actions
for comfort to relieve pain
now is the age to remember
we are one in breath and song

Hour of the Hound Wash – Jean Atkin
at Barton Court

Muck-caked, gore-muzzled hounds surge back below
the windows of the big house, and Johnny who
whips in this wild-eye, blood-up pack, slides off
his horse to lift the latch on the hound wash.

Swings back the door and sees each muzzle point
tuned to the breast-high stink of last week's chestnut hunter
jointed for them, mane still on.

Still giving tongue together they plunge down into darkness
and hit cold water. Rough coats are slicked to ribs.
Mud sails off from threshing paws.

Then each after the last, the hounds lunge up the greening sill
make their sodden leap out into kennels, spin water
droplets wide, then tug and growl and worry at the mare.

And Harry, gardener's boy, looks up from hoeing
to take comfort from the pack. He sleeps each night
in the lean-to by the kennel, still misses his ma

curls up on a straw mattress
drops off to the teeming river of them
baying and belling in his dreams.

Highly Commended *Indigo International Wild Nature Poetry Award 2021*

False Trail – Stephen Kingsnorth

Is it assumed land ownership,
forelock tug, the state relayed,
presumed as competent to rule,
divine right, guardians of fools,
timelords unchallenged, aeons through,
claim by custom, *droit de seigneur*
stance, arrogance, that so affronts?

Inheritance, child benefit,
maintaining order as ordained,
hunting by the profligate,
right classery in mastery -
it swims bloodred, bout the ring,
like slave trades, married, jumping brush,
a stag night whipping, lust full filled?

As mock the spectacle they staged
from colosseum to the pit,
bear-bait, cock-fight, dogs of war,
the circus tiptoe jumbo laugh,
like Bedlam wares for pokes and stares -
sporting chance means opportune -
how goes the stewardship in sum?

The cockles warmed by stirrup cup,
the bloodred pouring, mounted up,
coursing through the mad March veins,
with craft and wile claim trail their hunt,
all countryside their ground by rite,
gathered, carmine wrapped and warped -
should hearts beat faster, hart attack?

Vocation to uphold the lore,
status way above the law,
it's hoot and hoof, boot saboteur;
tamed game keepers hold little fun,
but brushed with death in foxy move -
pellets for winged preying stoop -
how cull the zeal - find mindful world?

Peregrine Falcon – Gillian Clarke

New blood in the killing-ground,
her scullery,
her boneyard.

I touch the raw wire
of vertigo
feet from the edge.

Her house is air. She comes downstairs
on a turn of wind.
This is her table.

She is arrow.
At two miles a minute
the pigeon bursts like a city.

While we turned our backs
she wasted nothing
but a rose-ringed foot

still warm.

Published with kind permission of the author

from **Auguries of Innocence – William Blake**
(original spelling)

To see a World in a Grain of Sand
And a Heaven in a Wild Flower
Hold Infinity in the palm of your hand
And Eternity in an hour
A Robin Red breast in a Cage
Puts all Heaven in a Rage
A Dove house filld with Doves & Pigeons
Shudders Hell thr' all its regions
A dog starvd at his Masters Gate
Predicts the ruin of the State
A Horse misusd upon the Road
Calls to Heaven for Human blood
Each outcry of the hunted Hare
A fibre from the Brain does tear
A Skylark wounded in the wing
A Cherubim does cease to sing
The Game Cock clipd & armd for fight
Does the Rising Sun affright
Every Wolfs & Lions howl
Raises from Hell a Human Soul
The wild deer, wandring here & there
Keeps the Human Soul from Care...

Baby Elephant – Clive Donovan

How could it not be loved?
 – This cute new baby of the herd,
Like the centre of an onion
Surrounded by concentric circles
Or the starring exhibit inside an auctioneers ring

Encompassed by the worldly eyes
Of wise old matriarchs
And on the edge, great tusky beasts
Who stamp on snakes, stick rhinos, and,
To bellowed shriek of trumpet, flatten tigers low.

And beyond them lurk ambitious hunters:
They will wait for the baby elephant to grow.
Soon enough he will evict himself to roam,
Risking his life and his freedom,
Gambling with butchers' trap and knife.

Right now he is useless to poachers;
Just an ordinary bag of meat and un-special bones.
His nascent precious ivory barely shows.
A cutter could not scrape from it an elephant in miniature.
A scraper could not cut from it a brace of dice.

First published in *Pennine Platform* magazine

The Water of Life – Heather Attwood

1000,000 Springs - life-giving, bubbling, spraying, foaming,
100,000 Waterfalls - dripping, showering, tingling, cascading,
10,000 Streams - trickling, bubbling, shimmering, shining,
1,000 Rivers - racing, eroding, meandering, flooding,
100 Seas - foaming, waving, dancing, swaying,
10 Oceans - swirling, roaring, circulating, thundering,
1 World - suffering, abused, polluted, dying.

Tasting the Wild Grapes – Mary Oliver

The red beast
who lives in the side of these hills
won't come out for anything you have:
money or music. Still, there are moments
heavy with light and good luck. Walk
quietly under these tangled vines
and pay attention, and one morning
something will explode underfoot
like a branch of fire; one afternoon
something will flow down the hill
in plain view, a muscled sleeve the color
of all October! And forgetting
everything you will leap to name it
as though for the first time, your lit blood
rushing not to a word but a sound
small-boned, thin-faced, in a hurry,
lively as the dark thorns of the wild grapes
on the unsuspecting tongue!
The fox! The fox!

Basking Shark Blues – Caroline Gill

No to the boats that tracked them down,
these gentle sharks with open mouths
fit for *The Tempest*'s shipwrecked stage.

No more, says the sea, *no more.*

No to the blood that stained the sky
when amber turned to drops of red,
all for the sake of 'catch and kill'.

No more, says the sea, *no more.*

No to the bay when currents churned
and giants flailed in harpoon-hands;
squalene and lamp oil scarred the day.

No more, says the sea, *no more.*

No to the bell when storms disperse
and silence echoes through the depths.
Where are the fins of basking sharks?

No more, says the sea, *no more.*

Everything that holds us tight – K. V. Skene

Swaddled in early-morning mist
cathedral-canopies of oak   ash   beach   birch
dream old arboreal dreams   spun
from a late march sun
trail markers emblazon our right-of-way
as breakaway breezes sift winter leftovers
uncovers things
we used to believe in
once-upon-a-time
far from the straight and narrow   forest
is everything that holds us tight to the world   is
everyone who ever welcomed us home
before memory slipped out of place
nevermore to be found accountable   rain
remembers the tears   the years
mourning what-could-have-been
and forest is aware
each successive footstep blunts our complacency
shatters our certainty of what is
and what isn't
the little truths
that scour us smooth
in time
high over the canopy
the thin sharp call of a goshawk
pitching and wheeling
as if there is no tomorrow
as if there is only hunger   longing   flight
right here   right
now

Galgo Español – Glenn Hubbard

Your past is a story I write in my mind.
You and the litter at your mother's dugs;
the rough hand that tugs;
the voice unkind;
the darkness, the rags.

When they open the lid of the box
you keep your eyes tight shut
while people shout
and someone bokes
as they rub your nose in your shit.

Days after day you wander the pen
peering through the fence at birds singing
from the branch where one morning *Flamenco* is swinging
till death stills the pain.
Crows descend as the sun is sinking.

At weekends you're freed for a while
to chase a hare across a field
till hare or dogs, exhausted, yield
to the will to kill or the will
to live. But the day arrives when you can't be fooled,

too familiar with your quarry's tricks.
The chase begins to lose its charm
when guess and outcome always chime.
You'll be dumped from a jeep by the side of a track
stunned by the perfume of crushed thyme.

A long day and a longer night.
Vultures appear as you weaken.
Unable to stand or remain awake you're woken
by a kindly man in white
and in two days you're walking.

A lady comes to take you to a place
where there's a *bowl*, a *blanket*, a *basket*
and something you love called a *biscuit*.
She strokes your sides, stares into your face
and before you know what's happening, she's kissed it.

Commended *Indigo International Wild Nature Poetry Award 2021*

Refugees – Patrick B. Osada

Escaping gunfire from the sea,
fear and blind panic drove them on
like any other refugees.
Without the lodestar of their lives –
away from the familiar –
they travelled unseen through the night
from far beyond the ocean's swell.

Singing, they kept their spirits high,
they passed Black Rock and Castle Point
to swing into the broad Porthcuel…
Beyond moored boats with jangling sheets,
the sleeping Manor House at Place,
they lost their way and chose Porth Creek.

Into this elemental place
of mudflats, long abandoned boats,
they moved in on a changing tide.
Beneath the overhanging oaks
where brown stream narrows, up near Froe,
the tidal waters ebbed away.

Caught up in flotsam, debris, weed,
the party floundered in the creek
as channel water turned to shoals.
Poor gardeners raised the alarm –
as sun rose on the carnage there,
of those who travelled from the sea,
only a handful still survived.

Now mouths are stopped – their chant has gone
and eyes are blind to helping hands
as men humped bodies to the grass.
There's tragedy, no respite won,
no refuge in this hostile land –
for those who've journeyed from so far
the sole lament is curlews' song.

A large pod of dolphins was discovered beached in the shallows of Porth Creek, Cornwall – 26 had died. It is believed that they had been panicked by explosions in Falmouth Bay during a naval exercise.

"The Hounds Caught Up a Cub..." – Frankie James

"The hounds caught up with a cub just now down there."

Casually spoken, an indifferent answer to my query,
the words are a death knell to my day.

The hounds caught up with a cub just now down there,
caught it up in their jaws and 'broke it'.

I am broken.
The bright morning is broken.

I had seen the vixen running, drawing hounds away
from her young, beautiful in the sunshine.

They lost her and came back.

When she comes back what will she know of her broken cub?
How long will she grieve?

All I know is my own sorrow.

I wish the speaker, "Goodbye"
which is a shortened form of "God be with you"
but I do not mean it.

The Sleeping Fox – Sylvia Clare

Like a fur collar
curled around the tree stump,
spine so neatly bending, a tucked-in tail.
Golden gleaming killing machine,
or perhaps a child's soft toy, stuffed decoration,
fashion accessory.
Wild fox, free, confident you can bask
when those around you fear for their lives in your presence
you need only fear man, human cruelty.
Specism, killers kill, human and fox, deadly combat
a hunt to the death, give as you would receive.
Hunting for pleasure or for life.

How to survive – Hannah Stone

She flicks through the newspaper in the coffee shop,
reads about how goldfish do it,
converting lactic acid to ethanol,
producing so much alcohol
they are over the eight.

Last night's *Blue Planet* showed
that Albatrosses, who stay loyal for longer
than the average African lives,
feed their chicks on the plastic meniscus
that prevails over sand eels in Antarctica.

She stirs a second cappuccino,
puzzled that having eradicated smallpox,
we die from comfort eating or foul water.
Some days she sweats for fear of fat fingers
pressing the red button, and satellites capture,
for posterity, trans-Pacific arm wrestling,
observes there are no lyrics
for *homo non sapiens*.

Omnivore – Jacquie Wyatt

On the death farm, amongst the graves
shadows rise, dart for darkness
sniff polluted air, look at us
like a hound its master.

They infiltrate my mind's maze,
pound ever closer
as my filmed eyes ask you:
what did we do when we realised?

Us self-inflating appetites, morons who
asphyxiated plants, poisoned insects,
killed our own kind because we believed in
this suicidal hierarchy of living things,
which flinched most, who expressed fear
in languages we recognised.

What did we do?

Listening to the Field – Kerry Darbishire

An unexpected northerly
    sets up
        a cock pheasant crowing like a rusty gate
            towards the ghyll
                wings ablaze.

I kneel to feel the warmth of his rest
    a hollowed bed
        of late season turf   brittle   still mouthing
            last night's   bluster   and   rain
                held on tongues of hawthorn
                    caught in hedges   wet

and spreading   quick as blackbirds   darting   from
    crab apple   to a sycamore grown stubborn.
        Exchanges in a twist of autumn leaves   scribble air
            hieroglyphs etched into sky the weight of clay
                old as land-keepers' secrets
                    letting summer go.

Wood smoke signals
    birth   life   death   lingering
        in this morning's shadows
            sheep-bone-cold   abandoned to the rustling fell
            when all is stripped to winter.
                A barn owl.   The last thistles blown.

Highly Commended *Indigo International Wild Nature Poetry Award 2021*

Wolf Moon – Emma Mooney

The first full moon of the year
hangs in the sky like a freshly
minted ten pence coin.

Her breath mists the air,
the camera heavy in her hand,
but she's patient…

She knows they're coming.

Bird Brains – Jan Moran Neil

We wonder what they think:
this gaggle of guinea fowl,
siren alarms of the dawn
en famille
stabbing through their bunched lavender.

We wonder what they think:
those leopard toads
stretching akimbo
through winter weeks
in their unchlorinated pool of green.

The yellow speckled
Christmas butterflies
flirting with the leaves
on their lemon tree.

The chaffinches that strike
the crust that's been stuck
to their razor wire
by brunching garden boys.

What do they think?

When two swallows
alight after breezy pause
with bags of noisy syllables

and drills
and bleating mobile phones
and gas cylinders
for braais

and outdoor living.

First published in *Red Lipstick & Revelations* (Indigo Dreams)
'braais' – S African fire barbecue

Urban fox – Jo Sanders

I've never seen a skulk of foxes
only lone ones
slinking in the garden
or foxtrotting along pavements
sometimes a dog
may bark in the night
at the shriek of a vixen.

At dusk or in the night hours
one visits us for food
first wary in the shadows
till its presence
seems like an offering
as we make our own in return.

I wonder if they dream
of their kin running free
in fields and forests
hunting voles and rabbits
in sand dunes and salt marshes

while they
live out of dustbins
or end up as road kill.

Small Men – Sally King

Bred in barren cages, row upon row
into the distance - boundless and bare.
Reared in pens, fed with grain, and guarded
by snares, traps, poisons, the calls of captive birds,
the bullet through the wing of a raptor,
the bullet through the heart of a white mountain hare.

More than fifty million tame birds
released from their pens come autumn,
to dash across unfamiliar roads,
to die in bitter frosts, these birds of Asia,
to be beaten to the firing squad,
to the line of guns: small men in breeches.

A single bird flies high, higher still,
away from the guns, trying to escape.
They all take aim - a living target.
Shots across the field. He falters, wounded.
A bronze arc across the sky. Falling.
Cheering. I did not cheer. For small men.

Winner League Prize *Indigo International Wild Nature Poetry Award 2021*

The Moment – Margaret Atwood

The moment when, after many years
of hard work and a long voyage
you stand in the centre of your room,
house, half-acre, square mile, island, country,
knowing at last how you got there,
and say, I own this,

is the same moment when the trees unloose
their soft arms from around you,
the birds take back their language,
the cliffs fissure and collapse,
the air moves back from you like a wave
and you can't breathe.

No, they whisper. You own nothing.
You were a visitor, time after time
climbing the hill, planting the flag, proclaiming.
We never belonged to you.
You never found us.
It was always the other way round.

From *Eating Fire Selected Poetry 1965-1995*. Published with kind permission Little Brown Book Group Limited

Here Is The Place Where Loveliness Keeps House – Madison Cawein

Here is the place where Loveliness keeps house,
Between the river and the wooded hills,
Within a valley where the Springtime spills
Her firstling wind-flowers under blossoming boughs:
Where Summer sits braiding her warm, white brows
With bramble-roses; and where Autumn fills
Her lap with asters; and old Winter frills
With crimson haw and hip his snowy blouse.
Here you may meet with Beauty. Here she sits
Gazing upon the moon, or all the day
Tuning a wood-thrush flute, remote, unseen;
Or when the storm is out, 'tis she who flits
From rock to rock, a form of flying spray,
Shouting, beneath the leaves' tumultuous green.

Mountain too High to Climb – Veronica Aaronson

Behind his colourful mask
the mandrill's eyes are glazed.
Once he was suckled,
carried skin to skin.
Once he crowed over
a cacophony of howler monkeys,
foraged for fruit,
on steaming ground.

In this dry landscape of olive trees
his troupe has been replaced
by a wattle and daub shell.
He's chained at the ankle –
a full stop
w a i t i n g
for his sentence to end.

My inner mother wants
to tear down the cage, unchain him,
reunite him with his family,
but the mother on the outside is worn thin,
held together with frayed thread.

As my three small children,
fed up with mandrill's face,
run towards an eruption of carp,
I'm pulled to chase after them,
find I've turned my back on the mandrill.

Incomer – Bob Ward

He's crossed a frontier
  between lifestyles
  at odds with each other.

He knew what winning's like –
  racing around in circles
  pursued by money.

Grey-muzzled now he sleeps
  backed hard up against
  solid security.

But since facing off a pencil
  sharpener, his nose
  pokes into everything.

So, I'm under surveillance:
  he dogs my moves, adopts
  my shadow as his cloak.

Such times we live in
  picked up from a world
  wildly chasing hares.

Empress in Wellies – Anita Gracey
(for Breda)

She has tunnels of love.
Warm milk is her hair
spring water her eyes
leftover dough her ears
a cow's amble her blink
billowing sheets her teeth
a nettle sting her bite.
Two pinches of black pepper are her nostrils.
Creevy cave her mouth
a kettle on the boil her tongue
a Ferguson purring her grin
the bells of the Angelus her laugh.

Every Friday in Church Square
she stands in the marketplace
under a marquee of white and crimson cloud
a crowd of faces suffocating to her
when she is so used to her
burly faced cabbages
or ladies of curly kale with
bouncing skirts of purple and green
smiling to the swallows waltzing for insects
occasional dog chasing whistles
or the cattle taking a farmer for a walk
mucky wellies obligatory.

Instead of a laughing twig in her hair
playing hide and seek
she now has a serious pencil tucked behind her ear
ready to do mental maths with a sharp buyer
who can't calculate the love of a
nurturing grower.

Sweet Idleness – Frances Sackett

(After *Dolce Far Niente* by John William Godward 1861-1922)

Oh yes, of course, my goddess wears these well.
I brought her many riches, truth to tell,
when visiting the Orient. That marble pool
she languishes beside was shipped to Liverpool
from best Italian mines. She dips her hands,
then lies and dreams on skins from lands
she'll only hear about when great men talk -
boast about adventures when they stalked
out animals for ivory and furs.

That passion! She's almost like a cat that purrs,
and in her idleness she must be glad
to know a man like me. I've had
the spoils of wealth. She's one. The painter's art
can only show what's there: munificence of my heart.

First Published in *Crossings Over* – Poetry from the Cheshire Prize for Literature. Also in *House with the Mansard Roof* by Frances Sackett (Valley Press 2022)

The Kingdom of White Stork – Gabriel Griffin

Along the riverbank he is
an old man rummaging for a fallen coin,
poking earthworm, grabbing field mouse, frog, shrew,
clattering toothless at his gawky mate with her
floozy scarlet-stockinged legs

Airborne he becomes
the king of Poland, painted with a Chinese
brush on Baltic blue. His wide wings sail the thermals
overcoming continents, bearing to northern lands
the soul of a poet.

The Kingdom of White Stork is Poland, no other country has more stork residents per square kilometre. In ancient Greece, Macedonia, Bulgaria, and Muslim countries it was believed that storks incarnate the dead. Pythagoras claimed that storks impersonate the souls of dead poets

Rich pickings – Jackie Biggs
(*Vulpes vulpes*)

A scream that rips a gash
through midnight streets
to call him at her coupling time
pierces your dream with her appeal for sex
while he silently stalks your suburban garden,
pokes his nose into your throw-away life,
rips rubbish sacks, raids bins,
buries his spoils for later feasts.
He lopes empty pre-dawn pavements
roams around dustbin alleys
scents his fecund mate where she waits
among fireweed under railway arches
ready to take him
inside their dark embankment den.

Calving – Valerie Bence

for Okjokull glacier, officially declared dead August 2019

Alone in the ablation area, among calving bergs
we are on the edge of things, silent
except for the crack and creak of ice.
Soon glaciers will be a fiction, whose ice tongues
many stories deep, used to move across land
with gravity and friction, would slip, shift, flow
become animate - make constant slow-motion movement
until they shear-off   roaring, drop into Mother sea.
The falling sends up cold steam, like a cow's hot breath
visible off her gravid tongue as she pushes.

There are few choices left - how to live,
how to die, what words to write;
on the edge of a dead glacier
it drip drip drips   becomes ocean

Animal Man – Dharmavadana

Deer-eyed, double-crowned
with tines, he stood glaring
through my windows
until I had no choice:

I unlocked the door
and stepped outside.
Snout to sky, arms whirling, wind
in his mane, he darted

into the oaks.
The Moon lit my way,
the trees groaned me through
and here was a glade

where smoke choked the air
and animals were laid
like leaves: stags, hinds,
foxes, badgers – corpses

pierced with arrows,
blown headless by gunshot,
skinned, quartered,
paws and faces seared,

yet somehow
their eyes still bright.
The King of the Animals
opened his arms and cried.

Commended *Indigo International Wild Nature Poetry Award 2021*

Shutting Down for Winter – Hélène Demetriades

The nest is smeared like builders' caulk
along the shed's eaves, whorl upon whorl
of a white and beige protectorate.
The rounded doorway welcomes the in-flight
of worker wasps fattening the young queens
with the apple crop.

Later, spiders wreathe cobwebs round
the palace door, striped abdomens
throb in the cold, narrow wings shiver.
No longer hunter-gatherers
the wasps crawl over the soiled meringue
of home, feelers, yellow legs and mandibles
fingering a sacred braille.

First published in *One Hand Clapping* magazine

In Meditation – Miranda Moon

silent in the space between breaths
perched on the next sound
inhale or chant
I hear bird song
my pause with their pause
we are united by our breath
mine yours theirs

with fox badger bird and deer
this land rises
in different sounds songs and shrieks
we people are not in concert
control from a self-appointed podium
seas of joy and suffering
course the years

the hare that runs free
does not pant or fret
but leaps and lands to rest
I have seen her there in height
glory sun on her brow
lifting her chest and paws to the final rays

the clear bugle calls a comfort song
says leave arrogance from our voice
use words actions
for comfort to relieve pain
now is the age to remember
we are one in breath and song

The Morning is Full – Pablo Neruda

The morning is full of storm
in the heart of summer.

The clouds travel like white handkerchiefs of goodbye,
the wind, travelling, waving them in its hands.

The numberless heart of the wind
beating above our loving silence.

Orchestral and divine, resounding among the trees
like a language full of wars and songs.

Wind that bears off the dead leaves with a quick raid
and deflects the pulsing arrows of the birds.

Wind that topples her in a wave without spray
and substance without weight, and leaning fires.

Her mass of kisses breaks and sinks,
assailed in the door of the summer's wind.

'We don't inherit the earth from our ancestors, we borrow it from our children' Native American proverb

Perkin's Farm – Patrick B. Osada

Trespassing. Secret borders of the farm
where boys from our estate would stray between
banked dead nettles, cow parsley and the stream.
Beyond the cinder bank the broken barn :

ramshackle cars, forsaken old machines;
nearby, deep water channelled over rocks,
splashing bricked sides below the ragged docks
and once, dream like, kingfishers here were seen.

Above the rocks the stream more calmly moved :
watery home of rat and vole, hunting
ground for adventurous boys with working
slug gun, catapult, stones... and aim unproved.

Then there was our Tree : a crazy willow
leaning giddily across the stream, an
unsupported ladder of green fronds — span
for the stream that flowed dark and deep below.

High in the crest (some said where lightning struck)
the trunk had split : a hollow gallery.
Here we perched, *The Boys*, full of bonhomie :
joking, boasting of girls, cursing our luck.

It was *The Muckers* tree — formidable
to climb, with bark worn smooth, nowhere to grip,
the sloping trunk.....and water should you slip —
crow's nest view : prize for the brave and able.

But then the farm was sold. Our Tree dug-up
when brook was channelled, dredged and gentrified.
Farmhouse and barn were bulldozed down. We sighed
for lost forever fields of buttercups,

the herds of Friesian cows, and meadow sweet.
When land was levelled – hedges all grubbed up —
school replacing orchard and pond's kingcups —
Our landscape turned to houses, street on street.

Today, more suburbs march across green space.
We concrete over land our parents knew;
but landscape should be children's rights and due,
yet more and more is lost without a trace.

Muckers – Gloucester dialect for friend or mate
Highly Commended *Indigo International Wild Nature Poetry Award 2021*

Walk – Ian Clarke

Ice feathered days warm to a close,
then out to the path to Heacham and Snettisham,
Stubborn Sand and Vinegar Middle,
grey pooling under the bridge.
Then to the sea bank, silt bloom and scrape,

where reeds skitter, starling blackened,
and that field he worked,
his scythe raw and sharp, wet with thistle sap.
He never heard mountains share echoes,
saw Dale, Fell or Valley

but stood against rusting wire
petted sad watery eyes.
But as that day burnt to a close,
there was totty grass, a leveret in her form
and swallows on a wire,

chest feathers still red with African sand.
He kept me close that day,
away from Nightshade's dying seed,
the creeks' running grave, sidestepping quicksand,
each stride scooping a dollop of mud

that healed as we passed.
Returning to that path alone,
past mudflats and samphire,
above me, birds' rain-washed cries overlap,
and that tree where we rested,

the wind still clinging to its branches,
now hollow, hording shadow,
where leaves pile and darken
big enough for a child to hide,
for the wind to cry unheard.

The Vixen – John Clare

Among the taller wood with ivy hung,
The old fox plays and dances round her young.
She snuffs and barks if any passes by
And swings her tail and turns prepared to fly.
The horseman hurries by, she bolts to see,
And turns agen, from danger never free.
If any stands she runs among the poles
And barks and snaps and drive them in the holes.
The shepherd sees them and the boy goes by
And gets a stick and progs the hole to try.
They get all still and lie in safety sure,
And out again when everything's secure,
And start and snap at blackbirds bouncing by
To fight and catch the great white butterfly.

Footprints – Mark Haworth-Booth

The doors around the yard are bolted shut,
the fences and gates enclose deserted fields,
a wheelbarrow is loading up with rain
and white picnic furniture begins to green
There are many reasons to close a stable – girls
becoming women, leaving home, money
drying up, divorce, of course, or serious accidents.

We once came to a hog-roast here,
the whole pig sizzling on a stainless steel spit,
pork slices served with apple sauce in baps,
a PA system, music, families,
those awkward conversations with neighbours'
kids and that slick-quiffed man of sixty
who goes dancing every week at Jive School.

Land was bought, the stables built, hard-standing
concrete poured, thanks – we heard – to a lottery win.
With horses here, young people rushing round
with buckets, feeding, grooming, mucking out
and hosing down, you wouldn't see the set
of pheasant's feet tracked in the concrete, neat
as stitching and clear as filmstars' handprints.

Come to think of it, pheasants are the only birds
we've seen here, alien exotics brought – heads poking
out of crates – to nearby shoots each spring, barracked
like recruits in huts and pens, later fed on grain
in woods, then driven towards the 12-bores.
I'm glad that pheasant marched across the yard
to make it hers or his – which now it is.

Snow in the Suburbs – Thomas Hardy

Every branch big with it,
Bent every twig with it;
Every fork like a white web-foot;
Every street and pavement mute:
Some flakes have lost their way, and grope back upward, when
Meeting those meandering down they turn and descend again.
The palings are glued together like a wall,
And there is no waft of wind with the fleecy fall.

A sparrow enters the tree,
Whereon immediately
A snow-lump thrice his own slight size
Descends on him and showers his head and eyes,
And overturns him,
And near inurns him,
And lights on a nether twig, when its brush
Starts off a volley of other lodging lumps with a rush.

The steps are a blanched slope,
Up which, with feeble hope,
A black cat comes, wide-eyed and thin;
And we take him in.

Return of the Clifden Nonpareil – Jill Sharp

You may see us, full-sail, at dusk,
the flash of our blue/black underwing –

wingspan wide as a small bird's,
as a child's hand.

Half a century extinct here, you could call this
our resurrection, though we've only flown the channel –

the space our forebears watched yours walk across.
We were your night-shift, pollinating

from summer's end to the start of winter.
Invisible on tree trunk, stone,

invisible through spring in the aspen canopies,
munching our way to maturity,

we flew as the nights grew longer,
never needing to own a name.

We'd greet you now in our own moth-language
if you'd step outside, and wait.

Clifden Nonpareil is a very large and impressively beautiful and rare moth.

Collateral Damage – Jean Hall

They were packed in like animals -
well, they were animals, or what was left -

mostly half-eaten carcasses, some taken
for cooking pots, some chewed limbs

strewn around, a bear blinded by a grenade
her snout severed by a knife-wielding soldier.

Only two survive: Lulu, a caramel-coloured
sow, weak and emaciated, her toenails

grown down the soles of her feet, due to lack
of space - she'd eaten her cubs, too

after killing their father to feed them
and Simba, a traumatised three-year-old lion,

scrawny, starving, rib-cage exposed,
muzzle protruding through rusted bars,

relentlessly pacing the damaged cage
seeking food, water and sanctuary,

abandoned to bombs, gunfire, hatred,
trapped between warring factions.

Occasional scraps of food are thrown,
soldiers taking selfies with bewildered animals -

all hostages of war, killing for territory,
beliefs, revenge, disease, desperation -

life of little value, certainly wildlife,
humanity at its darkest ebb.

Who now will pay to go to the zoo?

Long Man Dreaming – Claire Booker

Fish-tail clouds swim between my car wipers
rain pools swishing   back and forth   *quick, quick, slow.*
I pull up and park at the foot of the giant.

He's watching the heavens for weather
fierce in his newly breeze blocked body   thoughts lost
in the transparency   flying with geese.

Inside the carburetor   petrol chatters
its abrasive dialect of long-dead foliage. We sink
into blue haze. A brook has begun to babble

through my head. The leather seats are growing
back their bones; the walnut dashboard   sways   gives shade.
Fish will inherit the earth   booms the giant

as he sluices against currents with his upright poles
transformed into oars. They *slap, slap* between drowning
steeples   tractors floating belly-up   corpses

swept along in huddled herds. A mackerel shoots
rainbows across the car bonnet. Lobsters have tethered
themselves to the Pay & Display.

Their bubbles scatter like petulant bullets.
I rummage for my parking coins   find flint stones.
Is it too late to buy a ticket?

The Long Man of Wilmington is a giant carved into the Sussex Downs.
His chalk outline has been refurbished with concrete blocks.

Privileged Closeness – Christine Curtis

Making our way along a puddled path choked by grass
we find ourselves in privileged closeness to a toad

motionless in the sun. Like us, probably slowing down
in the October wind, its summer-fed, ochre plumpness

warted with ancestry, creeps away from our curiosity
no doubt on the lookout for a home to overwinter.

Behind us a mountain biker comes hurtling along
his eyes, we fear, fixed on miles.

All we can do is hope the toad retreats
into what remains of the *waters and the wild.*

Vixen as Queen of Flame – Bob Beagrie

The urgency of speaking without barking,
without screaming, from the boulder's top
and watching the yelped-word's swift flight

across the puddles of thawing daybreak
leaving what's left of the night in tatters,
and the slopping scents of herd and pack

spilling from the poor box of the morning
on a wind of shod hooves, rolling eyeballs,
lolling tongues, paws, fangs, riding crops;

the dawn is draped in flame, in fox fur
and the snowfield is molten gold, spoor
tracks across rig and furrow, the moon -

gnawed bone, the yelp-words are heard
like a flock of startled birds from the briar
before the hunt master sounds the horn

that says that everything is aimed at you,
or the bubbling red stuff under your pelt
and there'll be no justifications for dying,

from here on in there will be no thinking
but a filling of the mind with the fleeing,
the gulping down of stones, trees, streams,

become the spark flickering in greenwoods,
now, god-speeding, hot lightning striking
white whiskered navigations in thickets.

Dirty Business – Kate Eggleston-Wirtz

Heavy metal, music I think not!
No rock to sing, but sink and rot

to bottom feeders, gasping gills
native filters plugged and clogged - all those

the chemist kills with poisons fed
rise above the riverbed

as surface litter washed ashore -
blinded still, we still ignore

the dirty business, pigs to swills
detergency, cleaning clothes

our suits, weighted thick-skinned armour -
lift visors, see how sick we make Her

and every voice box stuck buried
cold in turbid water bodies dead.

Arachne's Glue – Corinne Lawrence

I
A step along the garden path,
and ghostly gossamer strokes
my cheek. A spider spinning her silk
in my hair? I shudder, flick it off, picture,
instead, the beauty of a frosted web,
its latticed lacework a fusion
of art and science.

II
Webs are a vocation, an uncut
umbilical cord her hold on life.
She sends out newborn threads
to catch faint breezes, ride
small thermals, find anchor points
on leaf or stem.

III
Her showpiece web is lab, salon, studio, home –
wine and fine dining on tap. Aged in sticky silk,
cured fly, a preferred delicacy, hangs
from her death camp web. Her daily tipple
is vintage dewdrop, encased in glue,
served from the prismed decanter
she has crafted .

IV
She can elude her own adhesive, abseil
air, walk tightropes straddling verbena
and honeysuckle. Engineer and craftsman,
she is obsessed with silver skeins and filigree fretworks:
an unparalleled Rumpelstiltskin...
or evil genius?

V
Arachne reads my mind: shrugs.
'Life is glue,' she breathes, her voice soft
as the silk across my face. 'Glue makes silk.
'Silk defines me. I dare you to bond
with me, human.'

First published in *Reach Poetry* magazine, Indigo Dreams

Chiddingfold, 1995 – Lawrence Moore

We wake, still taxed by our indulgence,
grit our teeth and face the dawn,
prepare to meet our antonyms
who gather on degraded lawn.
Patiently, we rev the Sherpa,
grab the CB radio,
check the stocks of citronella,
two more splutters, off we go.
Several stops for our compadres.
Almost feels like one big lark
until we hit the country lanes
that lead us down to Petworth Park.
At Petworth Park, they start their rituals,
caps are doffed by roadside cogs.
We strive to check our tempers at
the squalid state of hunting dogs.
They steal away by private exit.
Undeterred, we track them still.
The sabs split up - if we don't find them,
Chichester or Brighton will -
but we are sought as well as seekers,
labour to confuse and bluff
the watchful eyes of law enforcement,
waiting fists of local roughs.
For half a day, the different factions
hustle, jostle, shout and boast.
At two fifteen, it all goes wild;
the hounds, I fear, are drawing close.
We've got ourselves amongst it all,
we're trying everything we can,
we're sounding horns and barring gates,

whatever might upset the plan,
yet half the pack goes on unhindered,
baying swells before it fades.
Suddenly, the cold is bitter,
everything in darker shades,
but three fifteen, we pass a huntsman
slowly packing up his horse.
He jokes of having made a kill
but looks a little out of sorts.
Left to our interpretations,
everything turns out all right.
We head for home and crank the playlist;
till next week, our hearts are light.

Forest whispers – Lizzie Smith

This is the tramping ground of my Dad
where he picked gold mushrooms
to sell for beer money. Now it's crackled
through by dogs in the bracken.

In the thick of this forest you can pause
and try to catch it – there –
a moment of silence
before it's broken by the whirr of a bird.

Somehow you sense a buzz
know there is an undercurrent
of a forest wide web of roots
sending slow telegrams to each other.

Mini creepy crawlies gnawing,
fungus spreading the word,
behind a bark of barrier brews
a sap of sensory signals.

My skin is too thin,
I can't communicate with these old men,
only stroke their trunks and lean my cheek,
hoping to hear the whisper within.

Japanese Knotweed – Stephen Bone

A single female specimen,
no males were taken, you
survived wave drenched decks

to be bedded in Victorian soil.
An ornamental, clusters white
as Fuji's tip, leaves the shape

of valentine hearts
to compliment the rhododendron
and ginkgo.

Sinister geisha.
How well you hid your true nature,
no one could have suspected

your merciless roots,
breakneck speed of your advance,
the green putsch you plot underfoot.

First published in *Atrium* magazine

After Men – Martin Briggs

O gibbeted rook, O cock pheasant dead in the road,
O wood dove downed by a storm of lead,
O plundered owl grounded, O grouse bred for death on the moor,
O new-fledged sparrow fast in domestic claws -

what, no malice for bait-layer, poison-sprayer, cunning cat,
for gamekeeper, egg thief, speed-frantic motorist? What,
O skylark evicted, O scavenging gull on the wave-tip of waste,
do you find to forgive in your brooding ingenuous breast?

Limp hangs your beauty, O mute murdered swan,
prey to the energy of ingenuity of man.
All for our trespass who endure execution,
persecuted for being, put to extinction,

now as you flock, O resurrected birds,
why do you not blame us self-worshipping gods?
How can you forget, and your innocence sing
so wildly on uplifted, unbloodied wings?

What cawing, what trilling, what twittering, crowing,
what pulsing and preening must be now, enjoying
your transfigured element, beyond sacrifice,
O victims, all gathered before an all-fatherly face.

Below Becky Addy Wood – Dru Marland

By early afternoon our boats had got too hot for comfort,
broadside on, unshaded from the sun,
and Phil and I were sitting on the big ash log
that someone years ago had carved a long bench from,
and now the bugs were slowly claiming for their own.
Small heaps of dust showed where stag beetles had burrowed,
and every now and then we'd see an ichneumon
consider possibilities as it hovered over them.

With just the most perfunctory of warning roars
a Hercules flew low and fast above our heads
and banked hard over, following the valley to the south.
Its camouflage was obviously meant for somewhere else,
more desertlike than Wiltshire on an August day.

The silence crept back in. A buzzard's call was quite enough
to echo round this dome of sky, the pasture where the sheep
were huddled in the shadow of the tree, the idle boats.
And over Becky Addy Wood we saw a bank of what we thought was mist
blank out the treetops like a fret or haar. And then we smelt the
fire;
"Oh, it's the Amazon!" I said, and then for just a while
we watched the spreading smoke, and said no more.

To The Man Who Poisoned 420 Eagles In A Year – Julian Bishop

(Tubbut, New South Wales)

Did you watch gimlet-eyed by Snowy River as your bomb went off
while she glided on an updraft of warm summer air?

Did you smile as her lights dulled and engine stalled
five thousand feet above the ground?

Did you blink as her nine-foot wingspan swerved into a loop,
lurched into a sudden double-dip?

Did you beam as her landing gear seized up
as she hurtled towards earth?

Did you laugh as her portholes shuttered black, grin
as her tail fin skimmed a stand of plum-colured pines?

Did you cheer as her fuselage smashed on the mountainside,
as she writhed beneath a plume of brown smoke?

Did you joke to yourself as you raked through her debris
praying for signs of no life?

Did you strop a knife before you spliced her windpipe
to cut short her last hoarse squawk?

Did you warm your hands on her breast as you stuffed
her feathered wreckage into a burlap sack?

Did you stand back as the head was severed and skidded
into sharp claws of gorse?

Did your heart burst with pride as you piled the skulls
knee-high in your tumbledown barn?

Did you tell the court you felt no remorse while planes on fire
fell like rain from a cloudless Australian sky?

Blue Embrace – Marie Papier

He wriggles his way into the niche
where she hides

pulls her by the hem of her pearly skirt
into his swirl.

Her arms curl in lovelocks, unfurl
around his body in a tender hug

as he clasps her mantle, his jaw
clenched into her delicate flesh.

She fondles his ear, slipping a
limb through his open gill

deep   deeper still
suffocating her lover's plea.

His tail squirms, his body pleads
for air until he releases his prey.

Gathering her frills, the octopus
vanishes from his cold eye.

Blackberries in June – Deborah Harvey

Time's become a fox in headlights, not knowing how to get
out of the way, which direction to run in. Other days

it's a may tree in blossom, grim Miss Havisham of the fairways
holding tight to last year's fruit, and refusing to yield to upstart

elders barging backwards into a month not named for them.
Or a flock of jackdaws pumping up tyres in their rush

to distract the attention of a midday owl.
Or even ravens that think they're frogs, or perhaps

it's the frogs that are mistaken, I'm not certain.
Though who's to say how strange time is, if I've read

too much into not much at all but when solstice
finds me in the field and the temperature drops

a dozen degrees from one unguarded step to the next,
I call my dog close.

Commended *Indigo International Wild Nature Poetry Award 2021*

Hares by Borage – Lynn Woollacott

Blue starflowers line the allotments' track,
wind rush hums through a coppice,
pianissimo, like a lullaby in dreams.

I glimpse a glitter of dust, ears and grain,
sparkles of gold in paws and limbs.

And striding along the path
my brother beats a stick, carries a gun,
he makes beasts salivate and run rings
in frenzied bark, bark, bark.

Twitching noses high in the air
the hares in the setting light

      bound   captivate

           fly

dancers on the whispering ground.
They dart into a cropped field,
double back and back again, teasing,
then speed through a gate gap,
on down the path with chuntering pheasants,
on through the hedgerow
they leap, oh leap into their kingdom –
of golden field after golden field.

My brother and dogs fall behind, grow smaller
in the hazy horizon.

Mrs Magnificence – Eve Jackson

arrived, not as a photo to be pinned to a fridge, nor with detailed ancestry,
or in the form of direct debit, but as a grey cloud this family adopted
on a dull day when the tumble drier burnt out, the kids fought and bickered
and the letter that landed on the mat informed that benefits are delayed.

She swiftly proved there's no such thing as allotment glut, and in the confines
of their cul-de-sac no complaints arose as she bum-rubbed
fences flat. An elephant in the garden carried more weight
than a whole pond of prized carp or top-of-the-range stone lions.

No-one questioned her keep as she lopped branches, trimmed hedges,
washed cars, rocked the baby to sleep. When she swiped an ice-cream,
before a cry could be released she had showered all the siblings
with a rainbow. Daughters painted her nails. Starlings explored her skin.

Then, one day her trunk reached through an open window, swung soft
breaths over keys to play a dirge. Her head tolled, one foot
began to swing, tears cradled in a series of wrinkles. A low rumble
deep within. The temple began to crumble. Hyenas sniffed the wind.

The piano cracked at first hit. A grave dug; a shock of figurines, trinkets,
napkin rings smuggled out by neighbours under secret of night.
Their own grandpa agreed to walk with a limp. Petitions signed
from this unlikely place. A wind began to blow, trumpeting unease.

Grey pixels fell for a week. Doors closed. Mrs Magnificence left.
Posts were repositioned, fences mended, grass sown. Family and friends
    sensed
a loss the size of Africa. The cry of the savannah lingered as a faint
tremble beneath their feet. Strange trees grew with lush fruit.

Unpick – Lauren Colley

Shake us and we settle,
clinging to roads and railways,
clotting at a crossroads
where a town begins to grow, swell, spills

into the suburbs: two-up two-down shells.
Take down the curtains, the picture frames,
the slatted blinds, mirrored doors,
wrap the plates from the dresser

and the china cats. Switch off
radios, TVs and phones, wind
the cables to walls — unplug.
Clear the mantle, heave back the rugs,

pick the boards to splinters,
strip the paper with nails,
dismantle, heap, scrub, abrade,
scour to bare-brick bones. Step outside

to untaffle the fences, the hedgerows, the walls,
let the lanes go to pot-holes and the roads
crack above tree roots. Twist the tower-block
teeth from an aching jaw. Coil up

the motorways and unzip the railways
in rich brown streaks,
reel in the wires, lever up pipes,
pick out the pylons. Tie off canals

with practised knots, turn reservoirs loose.
Ask the bank-bound river to relearn
her meanders, enjoy her floodplains,
sprawl into lakes. Let the streams decide

their routes from the hills,
the ditches unhurry through the scrub.
Trust the water to find its way.
The land will forget the paths,

overgrow our snickets and gunnels
alleys and tracks, shrivel
into twists of umbilical cord.
Uncollect, degather, rescatter.

It knows as well as we, that humans, like sediment,
are time in falling, and before long, resettle.

Song of the Ghost Badgers – Jane Smith

Recognize what you did to us.
Centuries we survived your dogs and sticks;
You pushed us from our homes to make yours,
Only to end in this - a cull by government decree.

Remember what you did to us,
Not in cul-de-sacs named Badger Close
But in memory deep, fern fronds of time –
Engrave us there and say our name.

Look at what you did to us,
Our empty setts where spiders dance,
Tracks that mark our passing and our Passing,
Our pad-claw prints that melted into mist.

Cry for what you did to us.
Tears like sap that drips down birch,
Tears like rain on the forest floor,
Salt laments for us ancient departed.

Pay for what you did to us –
Wisdom lost of nature's ways,
Blind to the seasons, deaf to the wind,
You two-footed ones who trampled kinship.

We live on in the fronds and the sap and the rain,
Moving through the shadows on the forest floors,
Through the winds and the mists all around you;
Gone from the land, our spirits endure.

Raptor – Roselle Angwin

Life's hard enough even when you've money –
seems to me my mates deserve some fun.
And after all, it's hardly milk and honey
up on the moors, even with a gun.
The hawks, you say? – that's scarcely of our doing
if they *will* stray where shooting has begun.
It's grouse we want; not 'anything that moves'.
I think you should revise your views, young lady –
come back when you have something you can prove.

February 2019: there were only nine successful hen harrier broods in 2018 in England. Between August 2018 and February 2019, 13 tagged hen harriers were lost, all over grouse or partridge moors.

Home building by numbers – Teffy Wrightson

Stage 1

Observe the men walking, clipboard in hand,
past tiny cottages crouched low in the fields
hiding behind this hedge,
ephemeral buds of blackthorn snow
there's a black metal crow
foreboding among the daffodils

Stage 2

Observe the men push past barricading trunks
squamous crocodile, smooth reptilian,
rugged furrows sharp against flesh
their armour against the corroding years
May blossom billowing in the wind
wild foam on a stormy sea

Stage 3

Observe a green space where a soaring buzzard
spies for careless rabbit kits
to feed her hungry chicks
for the next generation
        the dazzled gorse beams back
        the golden sun's message

Stage 4

Observe the men shouting, metal clanking
iron teeth gnashing, tearing, chewing
mushroom buildings born from destruction
war on nature, trenches, craters
        sad eyed refugees
your heart may break

Stage 5

You hear robin song, beck babble, but
no turquoise flash of kingfisher
no longer splash of trout
willows falling, calling to no one
where is the dipper
who bobbed on these stones?

Swifts – Mary Robinson

We hear the screams
before we see them -
a chapter of hell's angels
flick-knife wings slashing the air

black-clad dissenters piercing
the street with their keening
risk-taking pitch

smashing the glass hours
of this languid summer afternoon

hooked on speed
they fly straight at us,
veer off at the last moment

keep up, keep up,
we are not one but several
we are not several but one

it is surely a warning - the way
they stake their whole lives
on the globe still working.

Atavist – Louise Longson

Up the lane where clay kilns crouched
in a heat-haze, I stand near forgotten
ponds, neglected by everything
save the strands of green algae.

Empty weed-filled holes
lie heavy with the cold urgency of history,
the pungent sense of another earth,

a distant time.

Thin, broken paths of wooden laths
layered with chicken-wire lead a way
through the sodden ooze
that sucks at my boots.

There is a spawning-ground here, now.

In ageing tree roots, somewhere
in damp, stagnant dark, there is a black-
blotched anvil head

that curls into a fire-streaked belly,
rests until nightfall, briefly forages,
sleeps again,

dreams dreams of ancestral endurance;
waits
for the healing of the world.

If – Shanta Acharya

If the universe had not been Love's creation,
life and light born in an unimaginable explosion –
                              we would not exist.

If the Milky Way and the dust of dying stars
did not scatter in space, in love's reincarnation –
                              we would not exist.

If the sun and moon did not send their rays to earth,
awakening us to worlds beyond our imagination –
                              we would not exist.

If our sky did not gift us with the gods of weather,
protecting us from space debris and radiation –
                              we would not exist.

If our planet did not revolve round its axis,
inner and outer cores locked in lovers' passion –
                              we would not exist.

If day and night did not daily renew their vows,
blessing us with light and darkness for our preservation –
                              we would not exist.

If water did not enthral us with the miracle
of creation, the beginning of life and evolution –
                              we would not exist.

If plants did not produce oxygen for no reason
except the pure joy of breathing in carbon –
                              we would not exist.

If every species did not have a purpose for being
here, their lives worthy of celebration –
we would not exist.

If nature's bounty and resilience did not go about
scattering the seeds of hope and compassion –
we would not exist.

If greed and ignorance, pride and power
stand in the path of enlightenment and realisation –
we will cease to exist.

Encountering the Beast – Michael F Gray

As I take ship from shadow land
my spirits lift from darkling haze
to answer summoning of seas
to resurrect my island days;
to honour monarchs in the glen,
and sit with seals in ocean bays
to bask on rocks in summer sun.

The Sleeping Warrior dreams my name.
The mountains knew that I would come.
The rivers rush to greet the sea.
The siren sea still lures me home
where Nature, deep within her den,
unconscious of pre-eminence,
deals equally with beasts and men;

where, on a virgin mountain climb
into the heights where heaven's born,
I chance upon a mother hind
who nursed a nervous, wide-eyed fawn.
And, as I watch in empathy,
a stag, with not a hostile eye,
maintains a wary watch on me.

Too soon does dusk demand descent.
The way leads down a narrow path,
and here I meet the Royal Stag.
There is no fear. There is no wrath.
I gently speak, show empty hands.
Eyes lock. Souls touch. There is no foe.
No gun. No threat. He understands.

His eyes have looked into my soul.
New dawn will shine upon us both.
He moves to grant my right of way,
and steps into rough undergrowth.
I bless the day that two paths crossed
and two souls sought to co-exist.
No hunt was on. No life was lost.

In all his might and majesty
there was no cruelty in those eyes,
no bloodlust in that noble breast,
but he left unanswered questions
and their haunting's never ceased.
Which of us looked on beauty?
And which of us saw the beast?

A Brock Geology – Jean Atkin

Night falls & fills

badgers pressing grasses

they feed & drink

piebald noses low

below, taste all the cold

red iron beneath their

they follow glint of mica

unlock the parish scents

behind their claws

another on towards

no questions

the dingle with badgers

to bent curves

& play, they trail their

to flow of brook & deep

then warming rocks

paws & pads

in their skulls

fling back its soil

then shoulder one

midnight & have

for their deaths.

Lamping – Kathy Miles

Night spiced with fox, with petrichor and loam,
and here, now, a gleam of torch and jacklight

as these men, eager as truffle-mongers
wild for the scent of fungus, delve and probe,

skulk and blunder in this damp hinterland.
Shovel-handed, they dig through earth and stone

sweating with their labour, and yearning to hear
the clang of metal when it meets with bone.

And he is snarling, slack-jawed, backing down
the tunnels, chittering with fear, his lungs

a bellow of air, his baited breath held
close inside him, human rank on his tongue.

His head's a zebra crossing, an unchecked
barcode. And in the dark he's jumble-loined,

lubberly with his fright, his body hunched
flat-bristled to the wall. Above they wait,

ready for that heavy wedge of muscle
as he bursts, white with spittle, through the soil

and the terrier scampers, lighthearted
as a boy freed by the end-of-school bell.

But truth to tell, terrier doesn't want
to punch above his weight, prefers the feel

of rat between his teeth, the slippery
ease and squeal as he locks to rodent throat.

But master pays his wages, in biscuit,
rich red meat. So down he goes, finds, fights, holds,

while men listen, dig, shovel, and the owl
throws caution to the wind with her alarm.

And up he comes, old Mr Brock, clawmarks
on his nose, half-blind and tamping mad,

dazzled by light, deafened by barks and cheers,
the shock of men and lurchers standing there.

He's caught, slung into a sack, face smashed
to keep him quiet, his legs tied tight together.

Tossed to the back of an old green pickup
and saved for later, for an evening's sport.

But earth will not forget him - the soft curl
of his body, the bristly nest of him –

and when these men at last are laid to rest,
will feast with relish on their rotting flesh.

First published, *Bone House* (Indigo Dreams, 2020)

Butterfly effect – Naomi Huig

I dream of a world where Earls are Common
and Admirals dance with Painted Ladies
while Jezebels flit and Sullied Sailors sit
in the mud where Fluffy Tits puddle
Clouded Yellows faze Cruisers, far
from Grizzled Skippers Monarchs dwindle
and when I wake the dance has stopped
where sprays erase colours in a wingbeat

Giorria – Marian Hussenbux

Mankind seeks power for ever and a day,
The hunted beast can claim no rights at all,
This ruthless world lets man hold sway,
All other creatures must remain in thrall.

The hunted beast can claim no rights at all
Except that she may live or die for us,
Thus other creatures must remain in thrall,
No cause to cry, complain or make a fuss.

Except that she may live and die for us,
The Irish hare enjoys no valid choice,
No cause to cry, complain or make a fuss,
Beasts suffer, yet possess no lucid voice.

Those Irish hares enjoy no valid choice,
This ruthless world lets man hold sway,
Beasts suffer, yet possess no lucid voice.
Mankind seeks power for ever and a day.

Cobra – Harry Owen
(Naja nivea)

Halfway along a rutted dirt track, down
to where waters meet, salt to fresh, the car
bumping and rattling slowly through dry heat
and sand, we jerk to a sudden shocked halt.

No zebra, this, but a huge snake crossing,
dust-ochre and deliberate: Cobra!

Not especially hurried, no interest
in me, he goes about his fixed business
of searching for a mate: it's breeding time
and thicket is doubtless where he'll find her.

No hint of threat perceived or offered,
no hood or cape, no venom load, no death,

this is exactly where he's meant to be,
at home. It's we who trespass, intrude,
we who meddle, yet he leaves us untouched.
Whether from respect or fear, I cannot move…

then breathe once more, relieved, quaking, creep on
in first gear, dust stirring. But wait – brake, brake!

Ten metres farther – fifteen? – she too glides
but from the other side across the path,
equally unperturbed (at least by me),
so sure of her beauty, leading him on.

Is she smiling? I could think so. Does she
watch him brave the dance floor, does she flirt?

Of course she does, as he, hapless devotee,
trails in her wake, bemused, befuddled, in thrall
to the same erotic music that I –
decades past – heard and hummed beneath the trees.

Midway along this rutted dirt road, down
to where the waters meet, all our knowledge
becomes serpent.

First published in *Acumen* magazine

Female Tawny Waiting – Kitty Donnelly

I wait with her, porch shadows as my shelter.
His soothing vowels hoot at muffled distance.
From distance they disperse to absence.

Her high pitched plea increases
to insistent screeching.
I hear her listening, her dependence,

her uncertainty increasing
with the hole in his response
until anxiety becomes her sub-song.

I understand her thinking: *what if he does not come?*
The cypress hollowing, as though lightning's
struck out its centre.

If I owl to you across the wood
will you still answer?

3rd place *Indigo International Wild Nature Poetry Award 2021*

Heralds of Spring – Liz Neal
Brent Geese on Milton Common

You arrive with the autum –
not in neat skeins
but raggle-taggle flocks of grey-brown feathers,
to spend the winter in sheltered estuaries.

Far from your tundra home,
you have flown high above the curling foam
buffeted by gales and storms,
your cries dauntless, resolute.

Prophets of springtime,
you gather in hordes
with ceaseless ronking and cronking
that tells of your Motherland.

And then you leave.
Your graceful wings
lift you high above the harbour
as you disappear into transparent sky.

Yet there is joy in our souls –
your haunting refrain remains
a symbol of autum long vanished,
a symbol of the coming spring.

Imperfect December – Seth Crook

A blown season of washed-up limpet shells,
cockleshell pairs, fragments of larger whelks.
Perhaps the rougher gale-battered waters
dislodge these tougher shoreline characters?
Some keen sea-life biologist may know.
Just as some canny engineer may know
why the whelk shells are only in sections.
I could form a great, ornate collection:
a hundred ways of being incomplete.
What am I looking for in the dank dreich,
hanging about with sandy-hoofed sheep who pick
and nibble faded seaweed for salt lick?

First published in *The Rialto* magazine

Common ground – Deborah Harvey

Freight trains still use this line but the sounds I hear are from
much further away, at least as distant as when this land was

grazed and turf cut for burning. The apple trees blossom for no
one now, asleep behind their barricades of brambles that are

impenetrable, except to animals that hold this land in common:
skylarks, muntjacs, badgers, newts, so many of them.

The allotment holders have put down rat traps and poison on
lots 20B, 14 and 15A, also the rear of 11B, please don't touch,

and trees are rushing up the embankment, they're trying to
burst through the railings, maybe they've heard a road's being

built across this land, and now they're planning, they're dying
to lay their shadows down.

Hunt Monitoring – Terry Quinn

we were cold and wet
and tired and empty
and hungry and late
and silent and what

we didn't need right then
was a Land Rover blocking
the narrow lane ahead
and what we really didn't need

were two women slamming doors
striding towards us
rain glinting off green Hunters
hands thrust into old Barbours

stopping ten yards away
while we waited for it
not caring any more
as the attack began

So sorry for stopping you
but we just wanted to say well done
We're so pleased you're doing something
People don't understand
Hunts don't give a damn about horses
they're cruel and brutal
The wounds we've seen
cuts to bellies from thorns
And barbed wire and branches
Fetlocks bleeding
I saw a twisted spine last year

Their ligaments are ruined at ditches
You've been up in those bogs
they ruin a horse's tendons
They fall over stone walls
And as to their poor mouths
Sorry we do get a bit angry
and you need to get home
Keep up the good work

and off they went
and so did we

Commended *Indigo International Wild Nature Poetry Award 2021*

Sparrowhawk – Neil Shuttleworth
(on my garden shed)

Sometimes chance and quiet chaos
Bring predator and prey together –
What do they see in that frozen frame?
I saw the golden eye
Of Nature's fierce garden,
The outstretched angel wings of death.

What beauty, what elegant, sharpened,
Tearing precision of design,
What a lumbering gardener staring back.
How small does he see me
In my helpless stupor, my silent awe,
Here in my slow-time, potting shed world?

Is it merely a question of scale
That keeps these few short feet between us,
Or am I saved by his disdain
For all but feathered game?

As if in answer he sits there on my roof
In the russet, blue-grey speckled garb
Of the raptor king he is,
Surveying all that's his of tamed suburbia.

And then he's gone, not a sound
But the wind through a merciless forest.

Always a But – Sara Daniels

A metal barrier rose overnight like a stinking mushroom.
Planted posts carried thigh high bars ring fencing our open green.

Stained glass witnessed the deed, raised no ecumenical eyebrow,
or delivered pulpit objection to this monstrous desecration.
For generations our open green freely softened hard grey tarmac,
a trio of shops, brick sky lines, parked cars and school railings.

I rant and seethe, enraged by bureaucratic decisions made
from computer images no bigger than a clump of primroses
growing beneath oaks and hawthorns at the edge of our green
where I patiently wait for a bus to take me to town.

But, to my shame, this irritation, inflammation, will scab over.
I'll itch, scratch, until my skin toughens, becomes immune
like most other people I know. I don't fight, march, fly banners
in the manner of men and women old and new, I stand in queues.

But, one day … … I may…

Dark Ark – Ian Huckson

The wild is dead
as Brock in shooter's trap,
as owl chicks fed a warfarin'd rat;
a last meal of the twice condemned.
Angler's rare catch slowly
suffocates in the same air
our children breathe in
and fated to fail to thrive in;
engines devouring the oxygen.
Flail mowers 'reclaim' lane-side verges,
maiming wildflowers, bees,
birds' nests, sapling trees;
the scourge of scampering voles
with nowhere left to hide.
Domestic cats trawl the last vestiges,
killing with the indiscreet
percentages of gamekeepers;
their appalling dark arts
creating vast stink pits.
Grassland deserts grow sour
on noxious artificial shit
and nauseous slurry pits keep
seeping mass extinction
into our island's riparian veins.
Innocent remains - mole gibbets -
hang as tainted testament to
(as rotten as) the darkened,
human-vitiated, soul
of the foetid, fenced-in countryside.

Bat – Jenny Hamlett

It was not the desperate flutter
of a bird, nor the mad bang
as beak hit glass –

something more skilled
a glide on steady wings
avoiding furniture and walls,

but trapped in our living room's
tiny space, when all he sought
was freedom and the long night.

Holding our breath we opened windows,
turned off lights and at last
became aware of a stillness

in the empty air. He was gone.
We breathed again, but sighed
for a moment's exhilaration lost

from our quiet lives.

Do Nothing, Say Nothing, Weep – Louise G Cole

Outside, I hear the vixen call,
a banshee wail from across black
Irish bog, a dog fox summons, come
one or all, and my shame breaks
into tiny russet pieces in the dark.

The loud tidings below my wet winter
window mean for sure, this is last
summer's cub, alive for only two short
seasons, her newly sonorous howl
rattling the garden's skeletal trees.

Already announcing her fertility,
she's too young, too small, too skinny,
too everything for a bellyful of babies.
I may be too late, but her cries
cut through the lies I've told myself

about nature's destiny and survival,
when my hidden autumn camera captured
the scraggy fox scrounging bird food,
parting single blades of grass
for fallen seeds, kernels of corn.

She made fruitless night-time lunges
at peanut-packed feeders hung high
for blue tits, dunnocks, siskins,
but I didn't intervene, resisted urges
to fox-feed, let her find her own way.

She's a wild creature at nature's mercy
not mine, I told myself. Ironic loyalty
to wild birds lay no blame on kestrels
for sad heaps of hunted feathers,
her flimsy fox frame always the criminal.

And yet here she is, malnourished,
howling my conscience to the moon
as she cries, not for my food-shaped
atonement, but for a bushy-tailed lover,
and though I can't help, I can, I will.

When I denied the glassy-eyed vixen
lying in the lane, carrion for crows,
cubs left starving all those months ago,
one survived on bird table leavings.
Now may she thrive, fattened by my guilt.

My Spiny Friend – Sally King

Darkness.
The sun has gone,
the garden vanished,
the shadows blotted out.
The night makes
the world its own.
Not a time for diurnal creatures.

But for night creatures,
with keen ears and noses,
the night's alive
with food,
with worms and beetles,
slugs and weevils.
And possibly,
even cat biscuits.

Something's snuffling
in the shrubs,
around the pots,
and, sometimes, just straight over any pots
that come between
a determined hedgehog
and its dinner.
A noisy, munching, crunching, biscuit splaying
messy eater.

Delicate, inquisitive noses,
small, wary eyes,
a frown if disturbed,
twiggy legs and dainty feet

that run nimbly across roads,
rather surprisingly picking up speed,
but not always fast enough.
In search of hedges no longer there,
my spiny friend, increasingly rare.

Meat – Mark Totterdell

Seeing the half-pigs hanging behind the butcher,
brain split between the cuts of them and the creature,

feeling the bawling pain of the calf-torn mother,
hard many-mouthed machine up against the udder,

hearing the pent-up poultry's undying clamour,
louder than birthday kids in a fast-food diner,

catching the final breaths of the shoal of silver,
mouths making countless zeroes that gape for water,

watching the silly innocent lambs that caper,
loving the life of them, and their sweet flesh flavour,

grasping, as trucks back up to the house of slaughter,
terror's a thing before there's a word for terror,

owning the seeping heart and the fatty liver,
seeing the face of meat that is in my mirror.

The Chequered Skippers of Fineshade Wood – Zoë Sîobhan Howarth-Lowe

Back from the brink,
secretly hidden in the flower-rich glades
and open sunny rides of Rockingham.

This summer sees a return,
a repopulation of this chequerboard beauty,
thought extinct and longtime vanished.

Location revealed and invitation extended
to explore the trackways of Fineshade Woods
and carefully protected calcareous grasslands,
once more alive with Chequered Skippers.

Nectaring on Bluebells and Bugle,
females fly low among the shrubbery,
busy egg-laying, while males perch among stems and leaves,
so territorial:
darting out from the Marsh-Thistle and Ground-Ivy
to investigate anything passing by.

Fast flying, fawn and gold Butterflies,
Sunning their wings by the False-Brome,
and sipping on favoured blue flowers.

Hugo The Hunter – Lyn Woolcott

I've been having
a spot of bother…

I met a man called Hugo
and he told me
hunting is his sport

Sport is for enjoyment
so what pleasure does he have?
Is it causing
fear or pain or death
that is the most fun part?

But wait
Another term is blood sport
So seeing his opponent bleeding
must be the most appealing?

For the other player
in the game
is the aim the same?
Is there fair play?
A good clean fight?
Perhaps a sporting chance?

Killing his contender
means he is the winner?
Should his rival
survive alive
would she then
have won?

Could he be
a graceful loser
or ever
a good sport?

And on saying he's
a sportsman
can he speak of
sportsmanship
or claim he's
sportsmanlike?

I must get back to Hugo
He mustn't think me odd
But he'll have to say to me
why hunting is a sport

Sapiens – Sue Norton

No one is really a stranger.
Even the lark, leopard or lizard
has the primitive streak in the embryo
that we do, and whether life

arrived in stardust, or came smoking
up deep-sea vents, to evolve a praying mantis
or a fungus that looks like an ear,
we know that we're linked

as the puffin is to the sand eel,
as the ant to the aphid it milks.
So, when seas turn toxic
with red algae, and dry waves

of sand smother farmland,
the question is why
sapiens continues to eat
with metal teeth

the forest's lungs, and why
when a Kapok groans and cracks,
does *sapiens* not flinch?
Hear the felled trees

thump, one by one, hear
the muffled beat of a funeral drum.

Elephant – Roselle Angwin
after W S Merwin

What shall we say to you and your kind
when we meet you in the blue beyond –
you great herbivores who could teach us

to live peaceably, who for so long
have done our bidding as slaves, you who
bury and mourn your dead as we do?

What shall we say to you whose faces
we mutilate, whose children we orphan,
whose whole family we've driven to the cliffs?

Shall we protest our ignorance as innocence,
tell how our great and growing god Profit
dictates and who are we to contravene?

Might we admit to our failures of imagination,
our poverty of spirit? Or shall we plead merely
that the world and all that's in it was made for us?

fauna – Mick Yates

it is june and the sun is hot
up on brackenber moor today
far away the lake district fells
shimmer in the hazy distance
the sun is high in the sky
dragonflies hover in the reeds
sapphire blue and emerald green
as swallows skim the surface of the lake
stealthily hunting for unwary insects
the herdwick sheep are seeking the shade
indifferent to me as i pass by
all seems as it should be
on this rugged haven in the valley of eden
a nesting curlew calls out a warning
as i trespass too close to its nest
a haunting cry empty and lost

When the Crows Disappeared – Rachael Clyne

The first time I noticed the ash
was no longer decked with cronky shapes
perched top-a-tree, like they do–
or did, I said to myself, *Cor, stone the* ...

Tree was silent. It always held several,
squabbling over crusts, beaked from lawns.
Even fat and gobby woodpigeons,
now scorn the bread, let it lie.

When we realised the crows had gone,
we knew without doubt
we were in thrall to shopping malls
and mobsters.

We knew we must shape up
grow feathers, claws and beaks,
or the eyes of the dead
would never close.

First appeared in *Molly Bloom* online journal 2021

To speak beaver... – Chrys Salt

What started as a pile of sticks
becomes wet fur.
becomes a Beaver.

Out of some otherwhere I make
a kind of gargling chirrup
mewling call.

His cocked head pricks, slips neck-deep
in the pond, pulls glimmering vs
of ripple through a mirrored canopy.

I make a chirpling
throaty warble   luring coo.

Curious he follows me along the bank,
fan of wire whiskers
dog-nose wet with mud.
Buck toothed, black button eyes
fixing my gaze.

I growl come-hither guttural cries
tug his sacred centre into me
on lines of light,
tune to a frequency
some atavistic consonance we recognise.

He knows my animal,
I his human heart.

Then with a wink of lustrous   black shone
muscled sleek   slap of flat spatula
flip and dart
of speckled iridescent sun

his ripples widen   wider
and he's gone...

Kingfisher – Kitty Donnelly

It was a sign: pure lapis on the post
plunged into canal sediment.

It surveyed its territory, paused & darted
under Lock 9, a featherweight

jewel flicked on the wind.
Returning fishless, its head revolved

towards the glass where I stood,
museum-frigid: my first live Kingfisher.

I should have tailed its poem
through the frosted dawn's distemper.

It was tempting me to follow it by pen,
to know it vivid & separate

from ossified kin: that feathered
gift of indurated velvet

with scratched black beads for eyes,
whose twiggy box I switched

for football cards,
unable to stand the cloy of mold,

too old to poke my finger in the rag-hole.
Now it had risen: fallen constellations

etched across each wing,
urging me to drown my laptop,

ditch my boots, flit with it
through the waterlogged morning.

"When one tugs at a single thing in nature, he finds it attached to the rest of the world." **John Muir**

The Cry of the Earth – Kathryn Southworth

While children plant their hopeful sapling
the giant redwoods are burning away –
the trees are wringing their hands in the wind.

Fire up the spaceships, our planet is twinned,
a new Earth waits to be found some day,
whilst children plant their hopeful sapling.

Bur air will be quiet with no birds to sing,
skies will be lonely at close of each day –
trees are wringing their hands in the wind.

Did the Fall start the day Adam sinned,
thought every apple was his anyway?
The children are planting their hopeful sapling.

Count the butterflies left, the pattern of wings,
fill the verges with wild flowers, let grasses sway,
leave the trees wringing their hands in the wind.

On the window pane a yellow leaf clings,
trusting the world won't – this time – betray
the children planting their hopeful saplings,
trees that are wringing their hands in the wind.

On The Importance Of Being A Tree – Sallie Durham

So
you
wanted to be a rat
in the school assembly
but they picked you to be a tree.
Boring, you said – just a tree.
Trees are peaceful and important, I said.
Trees are the breathing lungs of the world.
Trees are a one-stop motel for the world's birds.
Trees know nothing of city rats and their slicked-back hair.
Every tree is a living sculpture, I said.
Trees do not bitch or complain.
Trees are never homophobic.
All genera are welcome in the forest.
Trees do not vomit on pavements or fight in supermarkets.
Trees do not put bombs on planes.
Trees do not take guns into schools.
Trees have no religion. Each tree is her own goddess and temple.
Her currency is foliage and fruit and flowers.
You won't find a tree in Parliament, The White House or the Kremlin.
Trees do not leave junk on beaches.
Trees do not have sex on trains.
Trees do not, in fact, defecate.
Trees take all the nourishment they need from the living planet,
and nothing more.
Trees network their roots in order to protect each other.
Trees have a heartbeat; their blood thunders like waterfalls.
Trees adore squirrels and children.
Trees do not bully, troll or subtly undermine each other on social media.
Trees do not engage in toxic, narcissistic or passive-aggressive
behaviour.

Trees are majestic, but completely without hierarchy.
I have never heard of a single psychopathic tree.
Trees do not urinate on monuments.
Trees do not build new towns on old meadows.
Trees can outlive humans by five thousand years.
Trees do not get drunk then drive the wrong way up the
motorway.
Trees do not jump off bridges.
Trees do not mind what we think of them.
Trees never curse, not even when we kill them. They fall with
grace and generosity.
So wear your green dress with pride.
Your ringed wooden heart is solid and true.
Hold steadfast to the earth, stand tall with the stars.
You are more
than just a tree.

Highly Commended *Indigo International Wild Nature Poetry Award 2021*

Summer of no swifts – Robin Gilbert

Sometimes one wakes
to a bright morning, and a sense of loss:
the small diaphragm of Jenny Lind filling the theatre
to the very gods
with an unbearable sweetness;
the plaintive lambs regretful of an Eden past.

Even the distant cuckoo seems to call farewell.

So it is this summer of no swifts.

Where once, of a morning in early May,
the sky was suddenly
        quartered
    and jubilant
        with their untameable
    cries -
both exultation and affirmation -
there is an emptiness,
        that no other bird,
not dwindling lark, nor willow wren, nor thrush,
nor wheeling gull, nor buzzard's mew,
nor even the homely swallow, epitome of spring -

an emptiness no other bird can fill.

This poem was written over twenty years ago, and, sad to say, Cuckoos and Skylarks have since become a rarity in this area, even Willow Warblers are unpredictable and Song Thrushes scarce. So it is no longer only Swifts that are absent. The number of Buzzards, however, has increased. In the poem, "Jenny Lind" is a Wren rather than a Nightingale.
Originally published in collection *My Own Dragon (2006).*

Meadows – Geoffrey Winch

they've grown thinner
on the ground – vanishing
from patchwork landscapes
and urban edges – losing
battles for survival

yet underground   ants   bugs
and worms would still be willing
to engineer soils to fashion roots
to feed grasses and flowers

to entice butterflies to dance
as they always did while leaves
furnished and tinted
peripheral trees and hedges
until they flourished full of colour

where avian songs would sound
not only from those boundaries
but from the skies just to harmonize
with beehum and insect choruses

all to stir the hearts of humans
those lovers of meadows –
lovers losing battles
losing ground

The Stag – Frank McMahon

A raven's flight splits the rising sun.
A curlew sings.

Their scent comes through cracks in the sky.
He turns his head searching for direction
in the compass of his gaze, moves

beyond sight to lower ground
of streams and quags. He turns.

The crest of the hill brims with silent hounds.
Their breath steams, tongues wash the air.

Legs stiff as stone, he lumbers uphill
to find the ridge, bellows as if in rut.
The valley throbs with fear and lust.

Too many to resist.
A long bass note dies
in the chamber of his throat.

Masked riders drive the hounds away,
an entry is made in the hunting book.
On grass and ling
a darkening smear of blood.

2nd place *Indigo International Wild Nature Poetry Award 2021*

Fifty-nine days – Jane Burn

to dream venery
to dress like an eruption in a tweed factory
(flat cap, breeks, long socks with garters, waistcoat
and jacket, stalking boots, cartridge bag—personalised embossing
available—shirt and tie, with embroidered pheasants upon it)
to feel the thrill of being referred to as a 'gun'
to pretend that you are on an episode of *Downton Abbey*
to go to shooting parties and drink champagne
to use words like muzzle, choke, barrel and completing
to pretend that you are doing your bit for conservation
to stride about with your weapon cracked over your arm
to decide which size of cartridge you will use
(the higher the flight, the heavier the shot)
to have them beaten out from cover
to have them flushed, straight into your path
to measure the length of a bird's pain
(how much lead does a 30 yard pheasant require?)
to aim into the space of air before the bird
to pull the trigger just before the bird flies into it
to cut out their cries
(the ones you do not kill cleanly will die an long, agonising death)
to blast them from the sky
to send the soft-mouthed dogs to bring the bodies in
to eat or waste them depending on your desire
to hang each brace by the neck for up to seven days, depending on
taste
to pluck against the grain
to cut each wing as near to the joint as you can

1ˢᵗ October - 1ˢᵗ February are the official pheasant shooting season dates in the UK. The 2023 season will for last fifty-nine days.

Fox is the Land – Jane Smith

Fox breath in the frost,
Lung blast of cold;
Fox time stands still,
Fox time is old.

Fox trot on the tracks,
Swift under the skies;
Fox knows where to go,
Fox map is wise.

Fox dream in the night,
Moonlight setting free;
Fox is a way of being;
Fox soul is me.

Fox nose at the window,
Hunter's door locked;
Fox will overcome,
Fox will out-fox.

Fox love in the hollow,
Fox young in the sand;
Fox is in the people,
Fox is the land.

Commended *Indigo International Wild Nature Poetry Award 2021*

Hunger – Billy Collins

The fox you lug over your shoulder
in a dark sack
has cut a hole with a knife
and escaped.

The sudden lightness makes you think
you are stronger
as you walk back to your small cottage
through a forest that covers the world.

From *Taking Off Emily Dickinson's Clothes* republished by kind permission Pan Macmillan

Because of Rescue Dogs – Ronnie Goodyer

Because of rescue dogs
I have had friends in the darkest hours,
companions who became outdoor shadows
and learned the meaning of unconditional love.

Because of rescue dogs
I have been taught how to approach the day,
how to see places and objects with refreshingly new eyes
and to appreciate the possibilities of the mundane.

Because of rescue dogs
I have been denied access to cafes,
had to apologise to picnickers for missing sandwiches
and to Sunday walkers for water-sprayed clothes.

Because of rescue dogs
I have possessed hard-working vacuum cleaners,
had stray fur hiding in carpets and clothes
and mini-dog clumps under sofas and beds.

Because of rescue dogs
I have experienced the pain of ending life,
watch ageing take over willing but incapable bodies
and cried so long and hard in emptiness.

Because of rescue dogs
I have a life that is rewarding and full,
that has made me a person who knows how to love
and receive love in their uncomplicated world.

INDEX

INDIGO DREAMS PUBLISHING
www.indigodreamspublishing.com
@IndigoDreamsPub